To believe in the possible
when its possible.

From the poet that believes
in the soul.

Nick.

# BEING UNIQUE

Nicole Luck

novum premium

This book is also
available as
e-book.

www.novum-publishing.co.uk

© 2020 novum publishing

ISBN 978-3-99107-055-9
Editing: Hugo Chandler, BA
Cover photo:
Nemetse | Dreamstime.com
Cover design, layout & typesetting:
novum publishing

**www.novum-publishing.co.uk**

# CONTENTS

## CONTENT

To be content with oneself is the best thing.
To be content with the world is ever so difficult.
To be content with your partner is sometimes possible.
To be content with life is important, especially when things
don't always go according to plan.
Contentment.


## GENTLENESS

There are creatures in this world who are gentle.
They have the integrity and gentleness towards all creatures,
no matter what background they come from.
These creatures actually put the rest of the world to shame.
Such creatures are so gentle that it brings tears to one's eyes.
Gentleness.
To hear others, speak about such gentleness and the kindness
that these creatures have shown towards them makes one
proud to be part of this family.
To realize that the elements of the family have been sown into
oneself makes one appreciate life even more.

## SOUL

The soul is a separate entity from the body!
Have you ever felt like you are out of sync?
That feeling when you are more aware of things.
Don't be afraid.
You are becoming connected to your environment and to those around you.
Each of us is unique.
Some have the ability to read others' thoughts.
Some can perceive what another will say before they say it.
Some can tell whether a person is telling the truth or not.
Some are just more in tune to nature.
Some can smell, hear, feel, see and touch things and know what is happening.
Not always everything at once, but close enough.
I can hear what you are thinking.
How do you know this?
You will feel it or sense it.
We are all unique!
Each and every one of us is intrinsically connected, whether we know it or not.
I bet that you may have felt something but was not sure what it was.
It may be faint or strong, depending on what stage you are at.
Ever slowly increasing at various stages in your lifetime.
We all become in tune to our soul and to the world around us.
Each one manifesting their own energies to others and those around them.

# LISTENING

Is like an artist at work.
To listen to another takes your entire being.
To listen to what is being said needs to be finely tuned to
understand what the underlying message is.
To listen with all senses is hard work.
To listen is to give yourself freely to be there for those who
need it.
To listen is a joy and sometimes painful.
To listen to the integrity of that person's soul.
To listen to oneself is important.
It sets you apart from the rest.
Listen.
You might learn something new.


# DIFFERENT

To be different to the one next to you is hard.
To be the odd one in your family.
To be last is hard.
To think differently is hard.
You will always stand out as being the weird kid.
Being different and choosing to remain different is hard.
You must have within you a lot of stamina and a built in
belief.
You must believe in yourself.
No one will help you.
Stay straight and be truthful with yourself.
And all will be fine in the end.

## CHOICES

Humans should still be allowed to make their own choices.
Humans have the capacity to choose what is right and what is wrong.
With each wrong choice one learns and can make the necessary corrections not to make the same mistake again.
With each right choice one learns even more and can further improve oneself.
But let each human make their own choice.
Often, when one forces a person into doing something against their will, it only increases aggression or passiveness.
And neither of these attributes are useful to either parties.
Why is there a need to impose onto others what is right or wrong?
Would it not be best to set the example yourself and follow your own advice?
One's example of how to live in our environment will often enhance the next human to either follow or not; but the choice is still theirs to make.
Be wise!


## CHANGE

To feel the change within oneself is blissful and fulfilling.
To no longer be the same person you were six months ago.
To be aware that you have changed for the better.
To find routine life difficult.
You feel your inner peace.
You feel like a new you and you are.
The old one doesn't exist and it's too hard to go back.
Life is different.
Existence is different.
Do I like the new me?
Yes, I do.
But it's so hard to explain unless you are going through it too!

## SUPERFICIAL

To be superficial with others is hard work; to pretend that you are something else when deep down, you know that you aren't.
To watch how others are superficial among themselves and others, it seems so easy for them.
How can one be superficial and claim that they are honest when they are not?
How can you prevent yourself from becoming part of the crowd and yet remain true to yourself?
I suppose that this should be easy by being with true friends who are like you and who understand the situation at hand.


## LOVERS

To be lovers anyone can be.
But to be true lovers which is a deeper connection between two souls is very special.
It takes time, patience and compassion for each soul to develop into being who they are.
Souls.
This is the basis of true love.
To understand the other person, one must first understand oneself.
Thus, forming the deep connection between two lovers.

## TIME

Time will tell when we will be together.
Time is not based on man's perception, time is based on energy.
Time.
Time is a constant reminder of things that the heart and the mind must work on to remove the baggage which we all carry.
Time.
Time helps the soul to awaken.
Time.
Time heals all wounds if we let it.
Time is compassion.
Time is the soul.
Soul is time.
We just need to trust time.


## FEAR

Why does one fear life?
What is fear?
Fear is another emotion of being human.
To be fearful prevents one from becoming one with oneself.
Fear is the opposite of love.
To love is to be fearless of what life can be.
Love is the healer of all things that man fears.
So be love and you will see that love conquers all.

## CHAPTER

A new chapter is beginning.
A chapter in which the old has become the new.
A new inspiration of thoughts becoming a part of you.
One may ask why me?
One does not know, but just go with the flow.
Life is a mystery.
Follow your instincts and all will be well.
A new chapter has begun, and it feels exhilarating to be part of it.
We all need new beginnings in our lives.
It expands our horizons and makes us want to become at one with ourselves.
So, enjoy, accept and be happy!

## UNDERSTANDING

To understand another human is to first understand yourself.
We are all the same just unique.
To understand the thought process of another human is to understand their culture, their language, their religion and their family upbringing.
Humans are not complicated.
You just need to incorporate the five senses and you will easily understand them.
Humans.

# PARTIES

To be young at heart and party.
Some party all the time.
They need to belong to society.
To feel that they are loved and needed.
Party.
For some it's not necessary.
But ninety percent of society, be they old or young, feel the
need to belong.
However, life is not a party.
So be aware.
For the soul is not happy if you continue to go against it.
It will struggle and die in pain.
Be compassionate towards yourself and most of all listen to
your soul.


# CASHIERS

These are interesting creatures to watch.
Each so unique in themselves.
Some more alive than others.
Some more curious about life.
Some look half alive.
Some colourful.
Some plain boring.
Cashiers.
They see more things than most humans who walk through
their shop.
Wow!
To hear their stories would be a field day of knowledge.
Some don't care as they are just there for the money.
While others are there to keep their minds occupied and not
be bored at home.

# POSTMAN

Now that's a job for the wise.
The amount of mail one has to take and drop off throughout the day.
Day in and day out.
Come rain, sun, hail, wind or whatever.
The postman is always there.
They are human just like you.
They must see things that most humans would not give a thought to.
The stories that they must have.
Just waiting for someone to ask the right questions and to lend an ear.
The postman is human with feelings and needs to be listened to.
So, lend them an ear and listen to their stories and you might learn something about your area.

# BUS DRIVERS

Oh, the joys of being a bus driver.

To be responsible for all those passengers who come in and out throughout your twenty-four hour shift.

Oh, the things you have come across and probably wish not to see again.

The weirdos that pass your window.

The strange tourists babbling away and not really knowing what or where they are going.

The locals who think that they know everything.

The parents and their screaming kids.

The teenagers and their foul mouths.

The oldies who have no patience.

The drunks who throw up on the top of your bus and leave the mess behind.

The ever-increasing traffic of noise outside your bus that some days you wish you could just walk out on.

Oh, to be the bus driver of a double decker.

Such great knowledge that you need to possess to be able to manoeuvre through the narrow streets of London.

Oh, the stories they would tell you if anyone bothered to listen.

The tears, the laughter and the madness that you see happening in London.

The good and the bad.

But at the end of the day, you still love your job!

# TRAIN DRIVERS

Oh, the stories that you wish you could tell the public.

The tears of frustration when passengers keep the doors open just because they can.

The joy of yelling through the intercom to tell the moron not to touch that switch.

The annoyance of having school kids visit a museum somewhere in London.

The awe of disbelief of seeing someone taking a leak on the track.

The laughter of joy at being waved at by some drunken sod who can't walk straight.

The horror of someone who decided to kill him or herself.

To feel sorry for the pets who have to go on the trains as their owners think that it's good for them.

Oh, the stories that the train drivers could tell you if you just asked the right questions.

They are after all just as human as you.

## COURAGEOUS

Be courageous in this dark world of ours.
It's becoming increasingly dark.
All the negativity being shown on TV, news, people's
conversation, fears – all brings the negativity into force.
You must be the light.
You must show the world that you are not afraid.
Even if it's just you.
You must be courageous.
To have someone likeminded by your side would be ideal.
But they may not be ready.
So be courageous.
With love and compassion anything is possible.
Don't be afraid.
Be courageous!

# LIGHT

To be the light in this world.
Is rather daunting.
To be at one with the light is a wonderful feeling of
blissfulness.
To feel the change within oneself, ever more powerful.
Do not be afraid of this empowerment.
You are the awakened one.
The one who understands your hardship of life's experiences.
You have come a long way with all the pain and the suffering
you have seen and have experienced yourself.
You are you.
Your soul is grateful that you have chosen the light.
The love within you has grown profoundly.
Your compassion to forgive those who have tormented you, is
commendable.
To love and to forgive yourself is even more valuable as you
have learned to trust yourself with all your faults.
This is the light that you must share with the world.
Be the inspiration to those who think they can't.
Be the light that shines into other people's hearts and souls.
Light is love and what is greater than this!

# KNOWING

I am no different to you.
I am just me.
I am human but not.
I have just learned to accept myself.
We all can.
Through the power of time, patience, healing and compassion for oneself, each and every one of us can be who we are meant to be.
Knowing oneself is the essence of oneself.
The entity of being with one.
The knowledge that we are more than human is the essence of being one with the soul.
The soul is all knowing.
The soul is the driving force of who we are.
We just have to trust in our understanding that the knowledge we have learned with the ever silent souls is the right path.
But time will tell at the end whether we are right or not.
Don't be discouraged by the wrong turns that we sometimes make in our lives; at the end of which we all will reach the end of our cycle.
We become one with knowledge and one with our soul, our energy.
Trusting yourself is the greatest knowledge we can learn.
Knowing.

# INTUITION

To follow one's intuition is very important.
The sixth sense.
That feeling or knowing that someone needs your help.
That feeling that they aren't coping.
Being there, no matter how far or near is very important to
them.
Loving them for who they are.
Making them understand that no matter what, you will
always be there for them.
No matter how insignificant or huge they feel the problem is,
let them know that you love them and are there for them if
they need it.
No pressure.
But trust yourself and in time all things will be good.
Life is full of mysteries, especially when it comes to the soul
and the deep connection between two humans.


# CARING

To care for someone is to trust them with all your heart.
To care for someone who is afraid to show themselves is very
important, but it is even more important to be strong for both
of you.
To have patience for the person whom you care so much for is
very important.
To not exert pressure when you are impatient.
To be there when they need you the most.
To be open to anything.
To be aware of their inability of accepting any form of love.
Being patient and caring is what's important now.
No more and no less.

## ACCEPTANCE

To accept another is hard for some.
To accept a helping hand when the going gets tough.
To think that one needs no help is being afraid of being hurt again.
To accept that oneself feels less worthy.
But it isn't a form of weakness but bravery.
We all need to learn to accept someone's help.
No matter what we think.
Be courageous and take the first step into the unknown.
You might like it and your soul will love you for it.


## LOSE

To be at odds with oneself is a form of denying oneself happiness.
Why?
Why aren't you brave enough within yourself?
What do you have to lose?
Nothing really.
In reality you will gain knowledge and love for trying, even if things don't work out.
But that feeling of being with the one you love, be it friend or more; is the greatest feeling of all.
Your happiness is what's at stake.
Your soul will love you for being with the one who you are meant to be with.

# BEAUTY

Oh, to be beautiful and young.
To know that others envy you not only for your beauty but
for your intelligence.
Such a beautiful creature, both inside and out, not knowing
how proud your parent is of you.
To know that you can take care of yourself and keep yourself
safe in this crazy world of ours.
Love you!


# THE UGLY DUCKLING

The ugly duckling who became a swan.
To see the changes from unsureness to confidence is the
greatest feeling within oneself.
To know that you are a swan among swans and yet unique.
It's a great feeling.
To be confident and full of love towards one, is the greatest
gift one can have.
Oh! the ugly duckling has become a swan.
In its own right it has achieved, and it has its sights on
becoming more than expected.
That feeling of being one with oneself.
That swan is the envy of others.
Everyone wants to be like the swan but the ingredients are
missing selflessness, honesty, pure love, inner-peace, inner-
strength, belief in oneself that through time and patience
something good will come out of it.
The beautiful swan of elegance who manifests all good things
around oneself.
The swan!

# ROOTS

What are your roots?
Where do you call home?
Difficult to say if you don't know.
For the lucky, no problem.
But can you imagine not knowing.
Your soul knows that you belong to the world but as a human, you don't belong anywhere.
Roots.
The only roots one belongs to is where you feel your soul belongs.
But where is that?
Nowhere and yet everywhere.

# MASKS

Humans wear masks so that no one reads their emotions.
Why?
Would it be not better to be truthful to what we feel than hiding behind our mask.
Can you tell what a person is feeling or hiding?
People wear a mask for many reasons.
The fear of being open and getting hurt.
But we all know that we need to learn from our mistakes, no matter how hard or how terrible the pain is.
Don't hide behind the mask – it only becomes harder to remove oneself from hiding who you truly are.
Set yourself free and love yourself and allow others in.
Masks!

# SARDINES

To be packed like sardines early in the morning.
To get onto the central line where there is no air and having
to be squeezed like sardines in a tin, can be daunting to say
the least.
That feeling of no one being awake and each in their own
world.
Each thinking that by going in to work early that one will
miss the rush hour.
What a joke!
There is never a good time when going on the underground.
For some reason or another it always feels like rush hour.
Oh! the joy of living in a large city.
Being cramped in and not being able to breathe, let alone
think.


# NEIGHBOURS

We each have to live with neighbours.
Some friendlier than others.
The lucky few have no neighbours, but the majority have.
Some are friendly.
Some are plain odd.
Some are musicians.
Some are noisy.
Some are plain rude.
These are the ones who one must be wary of.
One just never knows how they will react.
Oh! the nuisance of having to live next to people who aren't
like you.
Be careful.

## INQUISITIVENESS

One must always be curious about life, no matter how
mundane or difficult it is.
Asking questions on how things work; always wanting to
know more.
All this increases your knowledge of wanting to learn more
by opening yourself and to become aware that life around you
is precious.
Oh! to be inquisitive about life is great.
It makes you more interesting and knowledgeable as well.


## MILKY

To fly up into the sky and everywhere you look it's white like
milk.
During the entire trip you don't know where you are because
it's so cloudy.
Not even the sun comes out.
Throughout the flight, it was all a bit mysterious.
The only thing that was alive was the flight.
The humans inside the capsule, not having a care in the world
about what is happening outside.
Upon landing it was the same.
It felt like landing in milk
All white.
Not knowing whether you existed or not.
What a bizarre day it was.

# PILOTS

Such proud creatures walking together with their team
towards the flight to wherever.
Men and women who proudly wear their uniform and love to
show their passengers,
how well they can perform.
Because that's what it is at the end of the day.
Being able to provide the best service possible from A to B,
and in one piece.
Thank goodness that they have no fear of being a pilot.
You definitely can't be afraid as your passengers have put their
faith in you.
Being able to fly the plane is commendable as it's no easy feat.
To make sure that you taxi out of the airport, past all the
other planes with their long wings, manoeuvring down the
runway, queuing and then speeding at full throttle so that you
can bring the plane up into the air.
Wow what a job.
And of course the whole process begins again when having to
land without an accident.
A job well done.
I'm just glad I am not a pilot.
I leave that job to you.
Thank you!

## CONNECTION

What is connection?
Is connection something where we are connected to all
beings, entities and universal?
Do animals feel the same connection because of their souls?
How do animals feel that connection with nature and how
does nature feel as well?
It's feeling the energy, time and space that plays a key role in
all connections.
To be connected to all living matters that are combined and
thus learning from each other.
The essence of unity.
Oneness!


## EXHILARATING

To feel overwhelmed by the beauty of life.
To feel the meaning of what the poem is trying to say.
To be at awe at the words coming out of oneself.
Amazing.
Unbelievable.
Where has it been all my life?
It's such a great feeling to realize that it's me.
That my soul is alive and that it is willing to share this
beautiful message.
It is so important to bring confidence to others so that they
can believe in themselves so that they can do it as well.

## GLARE

To drive at night with the glare of headlights heading towards you.
To drive at snail's pace because the fog has just rolled in.
To drive through the tall grass and not know if there's another car heading your way.
Night driving.
Give a thought to those gentle drivers having to drive at night as there is no other alternative.
Drive carefully my friend and let me know that you made it home safely.


## TIME AND TRUST

The 2 T's.
The essence of life.
That deep connection between two people.
Through time which is different in a regular sense; that spiritual feeling that we are destined to be together.
Trusting time and ourselves that we want to be together.
Trusting each other that in time we will be together because we chose to.
Our souls will be joyful and content that we trusted time and each other in wanting to make something out of it.
Love is beautiful between two souls.

## NATIONS

To belong to one nation is hard enough.
To belong to two nations is a balancing act.
To belong to three nations is odd.
To belong to four nations is again a balancing act.
To belong to five nations is a bit off.
To belong to six nations is awkward.
To belong to seven or more is unimaginable.
There is neither balance nor awkwardness.
It's just plain crazy.
To have all these nations within oneself must be hard.
But not really.
If you accept that all are similar.
Then you are off to a good start in your life.


## COOKING

To listen to one talk about cooking, makes one want to cook
as well.
To be a great chef in the kitchen is not always easy.
To know exactly how the food turns out, one needs an eye for it.
To have many years of practice to know how to cook well.
To have the smell being even more important.
Oh! to remember how your mother was in the kitchen
cooking up a storm.
All those wonderful aromas wafting through the house,
making you hungry with the anticipation of wanting to eat.
Mmmmm … can you taste it?
The wonderful memories filling your mind with images of
all the wonderful food that you used to eat when your mother
cooked.
Oh! how I miss those days with my mother.

# GREEN

To see something green, tall and beautiful.
Standing confidentially and proud throughout the many
years.
A constant reminder that no matter the hardship, one can get
through it.
To be either a loner or part of the group, it makes no
difference, you just need to be you.
Remain true to yourself and all will be well.
Oh! to be a tree watching over the family in front of me is a
great sight to see.


# COINCIDENCE

To believe that life is coincidental or planned; depends on
who you ask.
Life is planned and meeting people along the way, we can
learn from each other.
Some stay in our lives for a short period whereas others for a
longer time.
Depending on the bond that we have with that person.
What message do we learn from each other?
We have to figure it out throughout our lifetime.
Always asking the right questions.
Listening carefully.
Feeling through the senses.
Through one's energy, we can find the truth.

## INSTINCTS

Trust yourself and all will be well.
Do not be around those who aren't yet sure what their life's purpose is.
They will bring you back to where you were, and you don't want that.
Your soul is strong and at peace.
Be with those who are strong and balanced like you.
Be true to yourself and to your deep connected one and trust your instincts.
Be aware of those who want to use you for their own purposes without realizing it.

## SECRETS

To hold onto secrets is not good for the soul.
Secrets that have been embedded in the soul which every so often come out.
Deep memories that one would like to forget about.
Memories that are so painful but need to be cleared.
The past is the past.
And the present is the future.
What one did in the past and it was dealt with should remain in the past.
To delve into the past may help one to resolve the pain but not always.
Secrets.

## WHY

This is a very useful question.
Why?
To ask this question is to be courageous.
To know and to understand the answer is just as useful.
Why?
Don't be afraid to ask.
Maybe you might learn something useful.
Whether it may be about yourself or about someone else.
Ask and listen carefully.

# MESSAGE

We each have a message to pass onto each other.
No matter how small or large.
It's still a message of hope.
All messages are there to help us.
Being able to discuss, to listen and to process the information;
is vital for each of us to learn from.
And how we process the message is also important.
Be it by walking in nature.
Listening to music.
Meditating.
Colouring.
Focusing within ourselves.
Sleeping.
However, you do it … be aware of the message that you are
looking for.
It's not always straightforward.
It's not meant to be easy.
We each have to go through our own life experiences.
Be part of the story.
Be open to the message.
Once you understand the message, it's vital that you
understand the meaning behind it as it will expand yourself
immensely.
But do not worry if you are unable to comprehend it the first
time; it will come again but in a different form.
Our fellow humans.
Thank you for your patience with us.
Without your help in conversing with us, we will miss the
message that we are meant to learn.
Wishing you all the best of luck in finding the truth.

## NEED

The urgent need to see someone so strongly that it takes you by surprise.
That deep connection between two souls.
The connection that remains deep but slowly becomes content, knowing that the bond between two people will always be there.
To slowly remind the soul that life must go on, but that the bond still remains.
Trusting in each other is the basis of this relationship and waiting for the time and the future to bring us together!
Need?
Not really.
But trust in time!

## DISTURBANCE

The constant traffic in this house, disturbing my thoughts.
Its rather annoying, especially when the ideas come, and I
can't write.
I suppose my thought is more important than talking.
But watching and listening to people helps bring about ideas.
Always learning.
Always thinking.
Always processing.
All takes time to find the right words to write something.
Thoughts that hold the truth.
Waiting patiently for the truth to be told.
Patience is a great virtue!


## LANTERN

Thank God I can't feel the rain, the heat, the snow, the fog.
Or, can I?
In a sense I can't for I am a stone.
But if one can think from a natural point of view I am also a
part of nature and therefore I must exist as one.
What do you think?

## CHANGES

To watch the changes happening before your eyes is
wonderful to watch.
To notice the difference day in and day out.
To change ever so quickly and no one notices except for
nature.
Oh, how beautiful and yet feeling the change as winter slowly
begins.
Yet for some reason it's getting warmer.
The trees are becoming confused as are the animals.
But they know what's happening.
We just need to watch and learn.
It will finally become clear!


## INDEPENDENT

To be able to be independent is the way forward.
To gain the respect from others but also from one's parent(s)
is just as significant.
Once you have reached a certain age, society expects you to
be independent whether you are ready or not.
To have a parent who supports you is more important.
So be brave all of you who have reached the age where you
are about to go into the world to become your own person!

## EXPLORING

To explore the city by foot is one of the most exciting things
to do.
By walking around, one gets to see things that normal
transportation doesn't let you see.
To explore the city, the best way is to see how the locals live
and go about their daily lives.
Exploring can be done all over, not only in cities.
We learn by exploring and going through the motions of
wanting to belong as one.
But sometimes exploring allows us to build up our own form
of the person who we want to be.
How exciting it is to explore.
Wonder what is the next agenda on the list?


## DEATH

Death is only the beginning.
One never really dies.
Our souls become one with ourselves.
Entity.
Energy.
The human body returns to earth.
Dust to dust.
Ashes to ashes.
Let us be joyful that the spirit has moved onto a better place.
Waiting for the time to return again.

# REBORN

Even if you don't believe in coming back.
Just imagine if you could.
Would you not want to do your life all over again?
Unless you are happy with the way that you have led your life.
But no one is that perfect.
Unless you are God and that's you and me in a sense.
We are the ones who control our lives and our souls.
But in a human sense we are not the ones who are in control
of ourselves.
It's an illusion that we live in.
Only those who are awake know but others are slowly
becoming awake.
And in time they will learn the truth as well.
Life is interesting to say the least.

# MOURNING

To mourn for the ones we love is a human reaction.
Humans and their feelings.
But in essence we should rejoice for the soul that we know,
will continue living around us.
The energy or the spirit becomes a part of the universe and it
is always connected to us.
The soul.
So, rejoice.
Speak the truth and remember the good times.
The soul will always be thankful for the truth and the spirit too.
The universe is waiting for the energy to become one again.

# WAITING

Waiting for death.
Waiting ever so patiently for death.
Knowing that the time has come to leave earth.
To return to the universe to be with the ones who we have missed for so many years.
To leave behind family but being at peace, all that is okay.
Waiting.
The wait is nearly over, and your soul can leave the body that it has occupied for so long.
The body which has gone through a lot since birth till now, sometimes good and sometimes not.
Learning the meaning of life; accepting oneself and your faults.
The meaning of being a human.


# GIVING

Giving to others whether it be in the form of love or just being there.
Sometimes one can give through material things that one does not need.
Giving is an act of goodwill.
Giving is through love.
Giving of oneself to another takes compassion and selflessness.
Being there for others in things which they are unable to do for themselves is the greatest gift that one can give.
Love.
Integrity.
Selflessness.
Purity.
Giving.

## KINDNESS

To be kind to those who you love is to show that you care.
To show kindness to another who needs it, is just as valuable.
Kindness is equivalent to support.
Support in understanding that you are different and unique.
Such a great relief to be understood.
No need to be something else.
So glad.
Because I like myself.
And to be gently supported through your kindness.
Thank you!


## TOUCH

To touch another person is lovely whether it be a special one
or not.
As touch is one of the senses.
It's through that touch that someone is able to feel your
energy.
To touch and to sense that you are gentle and truthful.
We all love to be touched whether through a handshake,
stroking, hugs, unless you have never been touched lovingly.
Sometimes it can be done through harmful means.
Horrible really.
Such evil in this world of ours.

# SPIRIT

Bless O spirit on this hour of death.
Accept my father's spirit and be gentle with him as he flies among the other energies.
Look after him for he looks for the energy that belonged to his wife.
The spirit is not separate but is one.
May the spirit live in eternity, blissfully aware of what it has gained.
Maybe it will come back to learn something that it did not learn in this life.
O spirit may you be joyful and to see you sometime again!

# GENTLE MAN

Oh, my gentle man, how tender you are on this sad day.
Oh, my gentle man, how patient you are with me while I go through this human emotion of sadness as my father dies.
Oh, my gentle man, thank you for understanding me completely.
You have made me feel content and safe with your gentle support.
Thank you for accepting me for who I am.
I am not your typical creature.
Always looking for answers to my questions.
I like sharing with you as I know that you get excited as well.
You are very important to me.
Love you.
My gentle man!

## INSPIRATION

O gentle soul of mine, always looking for answers.
You inspire others with your gentleness and your calmness on
how to live life happily.
With your happiness towards life and openness.
You are one of a kind.
May your dreams and your hopes come true.
But no matter what; you will never give up, for your soul is
strong and content.
Be the truth and the light in this evil world of ours.


## HAPPINESS

To be happy day in and day out.
To show the world that nothing affects you.
To bring happiness to those around you makes you happy that
you can help.
To know what you are is a blessing in disguise.
Be content and bring forth happiness to those around you and
show them that they themselves can be happy as well.
Happiness within oneself is to be content and at peace with
oneself.
To know that you bring happiness to others is a good thing
for humanity.
Happiness.

## SOLITUDE

To be able to enjoy one's own company is an accomplishment.
Not only that you become intuitive to yourself and to your
surroundings.
Being on your own without being distracted by things
around, would be better.
To be able to enjoy your own company, helps to solve
problems that might arise.
Solitude.
The opposite is company.
But to be solitary is important for oneself, as you learn more
about yourself.
Being human and trusting oneself and listening to your soul.
All are important!

## GRATITUDE

Oh, what a surprise it is to receive something out of kindness.
It was so unexpected and caring of you to give this gift, that I
was taken back.
I was lost for words with this unexpected kindness.
But I was happy to know that people cared enough to help.
Oh, what a wonderful surprise it was.
Thank you for the gift.

## EXHAUSTED

Everyone is exhausted.
No one knows how to go forward.
A good thing that we are two; one for support and one for laughter.
To be exhausted because of the heaviness that one must do to get through life; the expectations.
The only way to get out of the exhaustion is to remove oneself out of the situation.
The experiences that one goes through.
Life can be exhausting.


## SNOW WHITE

Oh, mirror, mirror on the wall.
Who's the gentlest of them all?
You are, for you are kind, giving, selfless, patient and loving.
You have no fear for those around you and they may know it.
Just as well, but they are still asleep, and they think that they know more than you.
Be kind to yourself and trust that all will be well.
Nothing can hurt you.
Oh, my dear Snow White!

## FOCUS

Being able to focus on one thing or another is the key to success.
To focus on yourself may help you but give a thought to those who need you.
To remain in thought for those who need you; remain true to yourself.
Focus on yourself they say, but how can I when others need me just as much?
So difficult in a sense.

## FORMATION

The planet is amazing.
To one day find out that new islands have been created because of an earthquake eruption.
It's all amazing really,
How nature takes care of itself.
That volcanoes and earthquakes destroy the landscape while in oceans where earthquakes exist, islands get formed.
Oh, how amazing it all is, really.
And
Thank goodness it's the one thing that humans have no influence over!

## ENCOURAGEMENT

To be encouraged ever so gently is the nicest feeling ever.
To know that one is not alone and is being listened to ever so
kindly.
To lose hope in oneself while life is rather daunting.
To be trodden on while trying to be positive.
It's really hard.
Especially when everyone is against you.
Thank you to my friends for being there for me.
You have no idea how you have saved my soul from going
under.
In time all will be well.
This is the time when you need to love yourself more and to
keep your true friends closer.


## LONELY

So lately I have been feeling lonely.
That feeling of the loss of a loved one.
Knowing that the soul is in and around us; always feeling and
yet its human form is gone.
To feel alone and yet not.
To have good family and good friends near is important.
To be alone is a good way to find oneself again.
Don't be afraid to be alone.
In time all will be well!

## FINDING

Having to find myself again is a bit daunting.
Knowing that I am lost and that I have no interest in life –
rather frightening.
Having to find myself again and that excitement of being
alive.
Ever so quietly feeling one's energy coming back.
Finding oneself and being courageous after a tedious amount
of stress.
Stress so powerful that it knocked you flat.
It took you by surprise.
Keep strong and you will find yourself again.


## CHOKING

Do you feel like the walls are closing in on you?
Do you find yourself choking under the pressure?
Fear not for if you follow your intuition all will be well.
It will take time to find yourself again but keep your senses.
Do not follow in the same footprints as others before you.
Remain who you are, and they will realize this.
In the end we are all human and yet not.
What is the purpose in life?
Is it to hate or to love?
Show them who you are, and they may come to respect you!

## STORM

The storm before the quell.
The calmness, thus surrounding oneself while the storm blows around you.
Oh, to take cover while it blows outside.
To make sure that you aren't blown away by the storm.
Sometimes the storm inside can be just as furious.
Oh, be careful of your surroundings – never knowing which way to turn.
The storm.


## SHOW

Today the clouds are putting on a show.
Such beautiful pink clouds as the sun rose.
In between the rain and the wind.
The clear blue sky with the majestic clouds.
All shapes and sizes.
Dark clouds.
Bright clouds.
Clear clouds.
Stray clouds.
All rushing by for a show.
Wondering where they are going.

## REFLECTION

Oh, the time has come and gone, reflecting on one's past.
All we can do is go forward.
To reflect on the past will allow us to accept our faults, thus
allowing us to work through our past which only reinforces
who we are.
Be courageous and knowing that all is forgiven.
You are the light.
In which you will show the world that you are not afraid to
stand up for what is right,
even if it means to do it alone

## BURDEN

To take another person's burden without realizing it.
To be so exhausted at the end without understanding how
and why.
To know that I can feel everything and accept it because it
really does not cause much harm.
I know what I am, and I know that I can handle it.
To accept is to understand oneself intuitively; who you are.
Light, love and compassion!

## REMINDERS

To be reminded of the most important memory and to have
forgotten what it was, so sad.
But exhilarated, as I have been reminded what it was.
Such a great feeling.
Oh, how could I have forgotten it?
It was the most precious memory that has become a part of me.
It was purely forgotten till the time was right to be
remembered.
Funny how life works!


## STUDENT

Remember those days when you were a student and you had
to go to the laundromat to wash your clothes?
Oh, what great memories those days were when we went
once or twice a week with the old and forty minutes later; it
was all clean again.
Oh, the smell of fresh clothes.
Remember?

## SIMPLICITY

What happened to simplicity?
The art of living as we mean to.
To be at one with our true self.
To be simple.
Friends and family will appreciate the authenticity of being simple.
Why be the opposite of simplicity?
All it causes are headaches and heartache not only within oneself but in those around you.
Simplicity.
Are we not born simple to die simple?
Everything else is just useless.
A means of being part of something when in reality we don't always have to.
Think about that?


## SCEPTIC

To be sceptical about life around oneself.
To be sceptical about family and friends.
To have clarity in one's life for the first time.
To understand what is important to oneself.
To have the knowledge that things will be different.
But, maybe there is hope.
That in time, all things will turn out fine.
Time is a great healer.
Time is the opposite of being sceptical.
So, be patient and don't give into hate.
Because it can happen if you let it!

## KEY

The key to one's heart is beautiful.
To know where the key is, is very important.
To be the one who holds the key and knowing what to do is even more precious.
Oh, to be the key holder.
To have such responsibilities.
Make sure that the person who holds the key to your heart has a gentle soul, for only then will your heart be open.
Otherwise forget it.


## END

The end is nigh for a new century to begin.
For many souls the time has come to begin anew.
For others, the soul will continue going through life as is.
Whereas for others, you will become ever more intuitive to yourself and to your soul.
Your soul will know what to do.
So, don't be afraid.
The end is just the beginning of something.
Wait and in time all will be revealed.

## CLEAR

Such a clear beautiful day to start the day.
To feel the sun on my face.
To think beautiful thoughts.
To be one with the sun.
To see the frost on the grass and on the trees, reminding
me of that time where all things are frozen, as if in a winter
wonderland.
Such blissfulness.
To feel for those who live in countries that are always frozen,
minus their hearts.
What funny thoughts.
When in reality, I am glad that I am at home where it's nice
and cosy.


## BLOSSOM

Oh, to see the cherry trees blossoming, especially in winter.
To be cheered up instantly as the weather has been slightly
gloomy.
To be reminded of spring that is around the corner.
To anticipate the trees and the flowers blooming and
displaying colours for all to see.
Oh, how I can't wait for spring to come and uplift my soul.
To bring forth the light which is waiting to blossom as well.
But in the meantime, I will take what I can get.
Thank you, Mother Earth!

## NUDGE

To nudge a soul ever so gently.
To remind it that time and patience will always be waiting.
To have the courage within to be brave.
To be the first to make that move.
To be the soul who will take that risk to be courageous.
To extend oneself to another without fear.
Nudge.
We can all be brave, especially where matters of the heart lie.


## YOU

Who are you?
Are you like me?
Or are you your own entity?
The one who defines who you are.
Are you brave or afraid?
Are you loving or full of hatred?
Are you selfless or selfish?
Are you human or more?
What are you?
Only you will know so follow your soul and the path will
show you the way.

## FALL

To fall when one does not always succeed.
To accept failure is to have the strength within.
How many of us accept failure with an open heart?
To understand where you might have gone astray.
No one is to be blamed.
Only you.
For you alone are in charge of your life.
You alone are in control.
For only you will succeed or fall.
So, choose wisely!

## ALIVE

To feel alive is a blessing in disguise.
To feel alive even though your health may not be good.
To feel alive even if the going gets tough.
To feel alive when those around you are gloomy.
To feel alive even though sometimes your job is hard.
To feel alive when the weather gets you down.
To feel alive as sometimes that's the hardest.
To be alive and to love yourself first and foremost.
And then trust another,
Wholeheartedly.

# LEAP

That leap of faith within oneself is so great you wonder why.
That leap of faith that has changed your life for the better.
That leap of faith that has made you believe in the impossible.
The possibility of finally being on the right path.
The right path that has been waiting for you to find yourself.
Aren't you glad that you took that leap of faith?

# FINDING

Finding out what you are under a stressful event.
Where most humans would have had no clue on how to deal
with it.
To find that you have the ability to get through anything that
you set your mind to.
That your soul is with you a hundred percent.
That it will never let you down, even in the most extreme
sense.
To find that you are strong.
That you give strength and assurance to those around you
without them really knowing why.

# AWE

To be at awe in the universe.
To be reminded how fragile it really is.
To be one with all.
To feel the power if you can.
For you to look deep into your soul; you can if you try.
It's magnificent.
Darkness with shining bright stars.
All twinkling in their glory.
Reminding how precious we really are.
Awe inspiring.
To be part of this magnitude.
This universe.
Aren't you feeling the power?


# BIRTH

The birth of a new star.
The birth of the universe as we know it.
The birth of spring, summer, fall and winter.
The birth of a new cycle.
The birth of nature after a cold season.
The birth of a child.
The birth of new life in all senses.
The birth of true friendships.
The birth of many new things that haven't happened yet!
Can you think of any births?

# BRIDGE

The bridge of no return.
To cross over, knowing that you cannot return.
Would you want to?
Not really.
For you have exceeded your own expectations.
Bridges can signify crossing from the past to the present and
onwards to the future.
Why look back longingly or not, depending on your past
experiences.
But the present is where you should be at.
For this is what prepares you for the future.
Life!

# LEAST

To least expect something to happen out of the ordinary.
To be fully unprepared for the inevitable.
To fully know that it could happen, and it did.
All part of one's life.
The path of no return.
To not always understand what time has in store for you.
But it must have a meaning.
We are all connected one way or another.
Never fully understanding and yet a few do.
And that's the mystery of being a human and a separate entity.
Trust yourself.
Follow your heart and all will be revealed.
Always ask and one day you'll find the answer.

## FRAGILE

The connection between humans is actually very fragile.
It takes a lot of patience and understanding between one
another to make sure that communication is at the forefront.
To trust yourself in trusting another is to be intuitive within
yourself.
Fragility.
Fragility like an eggshell.
That's how it really is between humans.
And humans are not the best when it comes to practising
what they preach.
They are often, the opposite!


## BEACON

To be the beacon in this world.
To show the way.
To be truth for there are those who can't be for some reason.
They would rather hide behind their masks or their egos and
let the beacon fly by.
So sad for the light is pure.
So pure in fact that only those who are worthy shall receive
its pureness and its strength.
For that is the beacon of love and compassion towards all
mankind.

# CHEERFULNESS

I love watching people who are cheerful.
They are such beautiful creatures who make this world a
better place.
A place of harmony.
We need more cheerful humans for they remind us what life
is all about.
Life is about love and compassion.
Seeing and feeling the beauty from within.
They make other humans feel good about themselves because
people become too depressed with their lives.
Being human!


# STILLNESS

The stillness in the forest is deafening.
At first it was alive with little chirps and the rustling of the
leaves.
But within a few seconds all became very still.
As if both parties were listening to each other.
Each trying to assess the next one.
Trying to anticipate what each was going to do.
Listening and waiting.
Patiently.
Each thinking.
Yet not afraid.
For we are both very comfortable in our own entity.
Each one knowing who we are.
Oh, to be home again.
The forest.

# FLOW

To flow with time.
For time is of the essence.
With time, our knowledge may flow out into eternity, thus,
never to return.
So, we had better flow with it.
Time.
What is time?
It's that connection from the past, the present and the future.
The connection that flows ever so gently, full of inspiration if
one allows it.
To become one with time and all else.
Never knowing what to expect.
Such anticipation.
Fluid like.


# RIFTS

Cracks are starting to show in the world.
Tension among humans has always existed for as long as man
has been on earth.
Has there ever been a time when man was one?
In unity.
Why is it so difficult to be at peace?
To acknowledge the fact that we are a small entity in this vast
universe.
I do hope that the day will come when man is in harmony
with all living things.

## CHERISHED

To feel cherished as a human, is an interesting feeling.
To be cherished among friends, even more unique.
For not everyone feels cherished.
Some pretend to cherish you for they are after something.
Others feel cherished when they misunderstand you.
It's such a precious feeling of love among humans for it helps
to expand the soul.


## JOYFULNESS

To bring joy to others.
For others to bring joy into your life.
To watch others become joyful on your behalf.
To bring joy among those who need it the most.
Joyfulness.
It's only being joyful within oneself that you can do this for
others.
And to not ask for anything in return.
For that is who you are.
Joyfulness.

# GREATNESS

To be great is wonderful.
To have that confidence within you is greatness in itself.
Be happy that you have found the answer, thus allowing you
to have this feeling.
For without it, life is hard.
That feeling of being great.
That belief that you can achieve anything that you set your
mind to.
For that comes from within.
From listening to your soul and to your intuition.
To become one within.
We all deserve to feel great!


# ANGER

It's easier to hate then to love.
It's easier to blame others than yourself.
It's easier to find fault with things even the goodness.
So be the change.
Be love instead.
Be the one who says enough is enough.
Be the one who forgives.
Be the one who stands up for the greater good.
Be the one to accept the attributes of others.
Be the one to see that you can help change other viewpoints.
Otherwise hatred will eat into your soul.
And if not, your soul will always be grateful that you have
chosen love over hatred.

## HEAT

That heat of fire.
Which causes such destruction.
For no apparent reason, for it has a mind of its own.
Heat.
That intensity from within.
That anger towards all good things.
Why?
For what purpose does this have for you?
For you are good and therefore do not allow such thoughts of despair to enter your soul.
Become one with love and you will become calm towards all living things.


## NOTHING

What is nothing?
When nothing is nothing.
Is nothing that concept of time and space?
That energy that flows through each of us.
Or, around us.
Connecting us.
Nothing.
For without any thing there is nothing.
I suppose in the end we will be able to answer this question of nothing.

## SMILE

Be the first to smile for that sets the tone for the day.
Be the first to smile to a stranger for often at times they may
not have the courage to smile.
Be the first to smile for that shows that all is well.
Be the first to smile at the world for the world will love you
back.
Be the first to smile and to think happy thoughts.
Just make sure its genuine.
And
From the soul!


## SYMMETRIC

To be in balance.
To be symmetric.
To be exact opposites.
Not one thing is flawed.
To be perfect in nature.
Life is not symmetrical for nothing is the same.
Or, is it?
For we live in various dimensions.
Therefore, it must be symmetrical.
It's called being abstract.
To think out of the box.
We are allowed to do this for we have the choice on how to
think.
Otherwise why live?

# GLOWING

Oh, how beautiful the lanterns are glowing in the cemetery.
Such beautiful little lights flickering in the air.
Illuminating the stones.
Giving a beautiful sense of mystery about it.
Not at all eerie as they would want you to believe.
If it was not so chilly or dark, I would have stayed longer but
the frost was setting in.
Oh, how I will cherish the atmosphere.
Such elegance in it somehow.
Such silence away from the humdrum of life itself.
The graveyard.

EIN HERZ FÜR AUTOREN A HEART FOR AUTHORS À L'ÉCOUTE DES AUTEURS MIA KAPΔIA ΓΙΑ ΣΥΓ
HJÄRTA FÖR FÖRFATTARE UN CORAZÓN POR LOS AUTORES YAZARLARIMIZA GÖNÜL VERELIM S
CUORE PER AUTORI ET HJERTE FOR FORFATTERE EEN HART VOOR SCHRIJVERS TEMOS OS AU
SZÍVÜNKÉRT SERCE DLA AUTORÓW EIN HERZ FÜR AUTOREN A HEART FOR AUTHORS À L'ÉCO
AÇÃO ВСЕЙ ДУШОЙ К АВТОРАМ ETT HJÄRTA FÖR FÖRFATTARE Á LA ESCUCHA DE LOS AUT
AUTHORS MIA KAPΔIA ΓΙΑ ΣΥΓΓΡΑΦΕΙΣ UN CUORE PER AUTORI ET HJERTE FOR FORFATTERE EE
YAZARLARIMIZA GÖNÜL VERELIM SZÍVÜNKÉRT SERCE DLA AUTORÓW EIN HERZ F
VOOR SCHRIJVERS TEMOS OS AUTAÇÃO ВСЕЙ ДУШОЙ К АВТОРАМ ETT HJÄRTA F

# The author

Nicole Luck was born in Namibia. She went to high
school in Indonesia. She went on to attain a B.A.
in philosophy in the USA, followed by an M.A. in
hotel management and tourism in London (U.K.).
She worked for the Hospitality Group in 1998 and
Delta Airlines from 1998 to 2002. She has only
begun writing poetry recently. Her favourite activ-
ities are travelling, reading, writing and thinking.
Her special skill is intricate communication and she
has excellent listening skills. Her poetry is based on
her life experiences. Her poems deal with various
topics such as integrity, light, honesty, compassion,
being unique, nature, friendship, truth, love, time,
self-esteem and much more.

# The publisher

*He who stops
getting better
stops being good.*

This is the motto of novum publishing, and our focus
is on finding new manuscripts, publishing them and
offering long-term support to the authors.
Our publishing house was founded in 1997, and since
then it has become THE expert for new authors and
has won numerous awards.

**Our editorial team will peruse each manuscript
within a few weeks free of charge and without
obligation.**

You will find more information about
novum publishing and our books on the internet:

w w w . n o v u m - p u b l i s h i n g . c o . u k